T0082253

Dear Parents and Educators,

Welcome to Penguin Young Readers! As parents and educators, you know that each child develops at their own pace—in terms of speech, critical thinking, and, of course, reading. Penguin Young Readers recognizes this fact. As a result, each Penguin Young Readers book is assigned a traditional easy-to-read level (1–4) as well as an F&P Text Level (A–P). Both of these systems will help you choose the right book for your child. Please refer to the back of each book for specific leveling information. Penguin Young Readers features esteemed authors and illustrators, stories about favorite characters, fascinating nonfiction, and more!

Reindeer: On the Move!

LEVEL **4**

F&P TEXT LEVEL **P**

This book is perfect for a **Fluent Reader** who:
• can read the text quickly with minimal effort;
• has good comprehension skills;
• can self-correct (can recognize when something doesn't sound right); and
• can read aloud smoothly and with expression.

Here are some **activities** you can do during and after reading this book:
• Comprehension: After reading the book, answer the following questions:
    • What are male reindeer called?
    • What is the soft coating that covers reindeer antlers called?
    • How much food must one reindeer eat per day to survive?
• Make Connections: Reindeer calves leap and play together for exercise. What do you do to stay healthy and get exercise?

Remember, sharing the love of reading with a child is the best gift you can give!

*This book has been officially leveled by using the F&P Text Level Gradient™ leveling system.

To my editor Renee Kelly,
who has supported me through
success and failure in recent years,
and to my dear friend René Casilli,
who has supported me through
the ups and downs of our lives—GLC

PENGUIN YOUNG READERS
An Imprint of Penguin Random House LLC, New York

Photo credits: cover: beewerks/iStock/Getty Images Plus; 3, 10: Marcin Wojciechowski/iStock/Getty Images Plus; 4–5: longtaildog/iStock/Getty Images Plus; 6–7: Evgeniia Ozerkina/iStock/Getty Images Plus; 8: calvindexter/DigitalVision Vectors/Getty Images; 9: jamcgraw/iStock/Getty Images Plus; 11: Dmitry_Chulov/iStock/Getty Images Plus; 12–13: JHVEPhoto/iStock/Getty Images Plus; 14–15: Robert Kelly/500Px Plus/Getty Images; 16: kjekol/iStock/Getty Images Plus; 17: madaland/iStock/Getty Images Plus; 18: (top) destillat/iStock/Getty Images Plus, (bottom) Rumo/iStock/Getty Images Plus; 19: Olha Pashkovska/iStock/Getty Images Plus; 20–21: Tom Nebbia/Corbis Documentary/Getty Images; 22–23: karlumbriaco/iStock/Getty Images Plus; 24–25: pilipenkoD/iStock/Getty Images Plus; 26: leoaleks/iStock/Getty Images Plus; 27: Mary Ann McDonald/The Image Bank/Getty Images; 28–29: Nick Norman/National Geographic Image Collection/Getty Images; 30–31: FO Dommergues/Moment Open/Getty Images; 32: kertu_ee/iStock/Getty Images Plus; 33: DELFINO Dominique/hemis.fr/Hemis/Alamy Stock Photo; 34–35: bizoo_n/iStock/Getty Images Plus; 36–37: (inset) nechaev-kon/iStock/Getty Images Plus, (background) Евгений Харитонов/iStock/Getty Images Plus; 38–39: CharltonB1/Shutterstock; 40–41: © Santiago Urquijo/Moment Open/Getty Images; 42: (top) Saddako/iStock/Getty Images Plus, (bottom) JackF/iStock/Getty Images Plus; 43: pum_eva/iStock/Getty Images Plus; 44: longtaildog/iStock/Getty Images Plus; 45: Roblan/Shutterstock; 46–47: Bryan and Cherry Alexander/naturepl.com; 48: coolbiere photograph/Moment/Getty Images

Visit us online at www.penguinrandomhouse.com.

Library of Congress Cataloging-in-Publication Data is available upon request.

ISBN 9780593093108 (pbk)   10 9 8 7 6 5 4 3
ISBN 9780593093115 (hc)   10 9 8 7 6 5 4 3 2 1

PENGUIN YOUNG READERS

LEVEL

4

FLUENT
READER

Reindeer

ON THE MOVE!

by Ginjer L. Clarke

Can reindeer really fly? No, not without Santa's magic. But they can run so fast that they look like they are flying across the snow.

Zoom! This herd of reindeer gallops up to 50 miles per hour—as fast as a car. They stir up a giant cloud of dust, and they make a lot of noise. What is all the fuss about? And where are they going in such a hurry?

It is fall in the Arctic. The reindeer are migrating, or moving from one place to another, before winter comes. They are always on the move to find tasty plants to eat. Some reindeer travel thousands of miles every year—farther than any other land mammal.

A group of migrating reindeer can be small or huge. *Rumble! Rumble!* Thousands of running reindeer shake the ground. It feels like an earthquake when they go by!

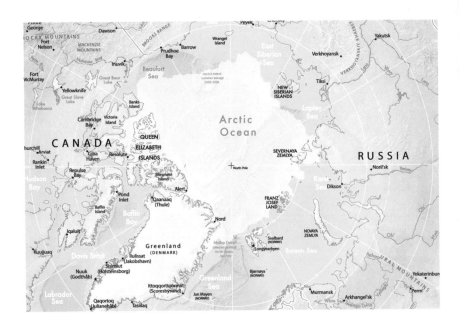

Reindeer have to work hard to find food in their frozen home. They live on the land all around the North Pole, called the Arctic tundra. This includes the most northern parts of North America, Europe, and Russia.

North American reindeer are a little bigger than European ones and are called caribou (say: CARE-uh-boo). They roam all over Alaska, Canada, and Greenland.

Both types of reindeer have awesome antlers. Male reindeer have antlers about four feet long, weighing more than 30 pounds. That is about the size of an average toddler!

The antlers are slender with branches at the top, like a tree. The males also have a short, shovel-shaped antler sticking out of their forehead! Reindeer are the only type of deer where the females have antlers, too. A female's antlers are about half as big as a male's.

Both male and female reindeer use their antlers to fight over who gets to eat in the best feeding spots. But the males, called bulls, also use them to battle over the females, called cows.

Then the bulls shed their antlers after mating. They grow a new, larger set each year. Cows keep their antlers until spring, after they give birth to their babies, called calves.

In winter, the Arctic tundra is covered in deep snow. Now reindeer do not *look* for food—they *sniff* for it. This reindeer smells something under the snow. *Scratch!* She uses her sharp hooves to uncover some reindeer moss.

Reindeer eat leaves, berries, and grasses during the rest of the year. But reindeer moss, also called caribou lichen (say: LYE-kin), is almost the only food that survives in the extreme winter cold. It grows where no other plants can. Reindeer are one of very few animals that eat it. The moss even looks like tiny reindeer antlers!

Just like their food, reindeer can survive the cold. Their thick fur has double layers to keep them warm and dry, even in a blizzard. Their wide, two-toed hooves act like snowshoes to keep them from sinking in the deep snow.

Reindeer's noses work like heaters to warm the freezing air before it goes into their lungs. Fun fact: Reindeer have a lot of blood vessels in their noses that sometimes make them look rosy. So that may be how the story of Rudolph the Red-Nosed Reindeer got started!

In April, the weather slowly starts to get warmer. The reindeer are ready to move north again. They migrate in a long line. The older cows lead the way.

Splash! The reindeer jump into an icy, rushing river. They paddle against the

current with their big hooves. The hollow hairs in their fur trap air and help them float. After they cross the river, they keep running through the snow and over mountains.

The reindeer stop for a snack. But they have to watch out for danger. Arctic wolves will follow reindeer for hundreds of miles in search of a meal.

One cow senses that the wolves are getting closer. *Huff! Puff!* She snorts and paws at the snow to tell the wolves to back off. *Jump!* She rears up on her back legs and gives off a scent from her ankles. This smell lets the other reindeer know that danger is nearby.

Suddenly, the wolves pounce! *Whoosh!*
The reindeer take off running. They
move together—like a school of fish.
The wolves back off. They do not dare
come too close. One kick from a reindeer
could break a wolf's bones.

The reindeer are so fast that they outrun the wolves. The wolf pack gives up, but they will be back. They follow the herd slowly, waiting for a sick, tired, or young reindeer to fall behind.

The herd travels for weeks and leaves the wolves far behind. The tired reindeer can finally rest. They have found a quiet spot to settle down where the tundra meets the Arctic Ocean.

Finally, it is spring! The mother cows are ready to have their babies. Many of them already have one-year-old reindeer, called yearlings. These yearlings will have to find their own food after the new babies are born. But for now, the herd rests together.

One cow quickly gives birth to her small, slippery calf. The calf has patchy fur and short, stubby antlers. The mother nods her head at the calf, telling it to follow her.

The calf stands up and wobbles. It is able to walk in just a few minutes. By the end of the day, it can run in circles. It is already faster than a wolf!

All the mother cows give birth within a few days. *Wheee!* The calves leap and play together for exercise. Even the mothers jump with joy!

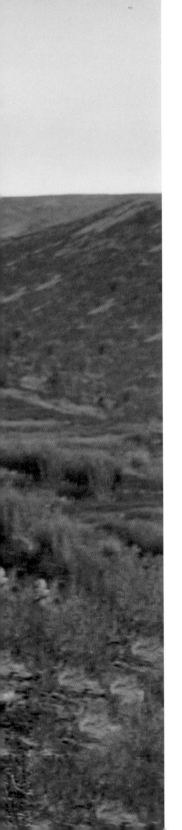

The calves drink
their mothers' rich
milk so they can grow.
The little calves need
to be strong. And they
must stick close to
their mothers. Many
dangers lie ahead.

Grunt! One mother
calls to her calf. *Bleat!*
The calf answers back.
They practice calling
so they will recognize
each other in the herd.
Soon, they will be on
the move again.

31

Now it is summer in the Arctic. The days are warm and long, because the sun never sets. And the reindeer never stop moving, except for very short rest breaks. The bulls have joined the cows and calves.

All of the bulls' antlers have grown larger. They are covered in a soft coating called velvet that helps the antlers grow quickly. *Rub! Scrub!* The bulls scrape off the velvet by rubbing against trees.

Their antlers are ready for another fall fighting season.

The herd is noisy. The cows and calves grunt to each other. All the reindeer rip and chew their food. And the reindeer's ankles make popping sounds while they walk. *Click! Clack!* This odd sound may help the herd stay together.

But wait! They hear another noise. A group of creatures is following the herd. This time it is something tiny—and annoying.

Buzz! Buzz! The mosquitoes are coming! The tundra is filled with small ponds and lakes after the snow melts. Mosquitoes lay their eggs in this water.

The eggs hatch all at once as the temperature rises. *Billions* of mosquitoes swarm everywhere, forming big black clouds. These annoying bugs bite the

reindeer. Together, they can suck a whole cup of blood from a reindeer in just one day!

Surprisingly, more mosquitoes fly around the tundra in summer than anywhere else in the world. *Yikes!*

Biting bugs are one reason why reindeer move constantly. They are looking for a cooler, breezier place with fewer mosquitoes.

The reindeer also wander around to eat as much food as they can. *Crunch! Munch!* They nibble on grasses, shrubs, and leaves. One reindeer has to eat about 15 pounds of food per day to survive. That is like if you ate 60 quarter-pound burgers in a day!

The reindeer eat a lot, but they are also trying to keep from being eaten. Besides mosquitoes, black flies, botflies, and warble flies all attack the reindeer. They even get in the reindeer's noses and eyes and dig into their skin. *Yuck!*

Sometimes the reindeer go a little crazy from all this biting. *Stampede!* The reindeer dash away as fast as they can to try to outrun the pesky insects. They head for the mountains to the south.

Some reindeer cannot keep up with the fast pace. Older reindeer often get left behind. Many Arctic animals, including grizzly and polar bears, eagles, foxes, and wolverines, prey on weak or dead reindeer.

Chomp! A wolverine eats a dead reindeer. Its strong jaws can even break bones. Some eagles will also eat reindeer antlers and bones. And mice use the leftover fur to line their nests. Nothing goes to waste in the Arctic.

People living in the Arctic also depend on the reindeer to survive in this harsh place. Native people have hunted and herded reindeer for many thousands of years.

They use the reindeer for meat and milk. They make clothing, tents, and bedding from reindeer skins. And they turn reindeer bones and antlers into knives, tools, and fishhooks.

The native people of the Arctic use every part of the reindeer they hunt.

Native people also used reindeer for travel long ago. Reindeer really can pull sleighs—just like in the story of Santa and his reindeer team delivering toys on Christmas Eve! But reindeer herders only used one or two reindeer to pull their sleds.

A pair of bull reindeer are so strong that they can pull loads of about 500 pounds for up to 40 miles per day. Today, many people living in the Arctic use snowmobiles for transportation instead of reindeer.

The temperature drops suddenly in September. Snow starts to fall fast. The reindeer head farther south in smaller groups.

Winter is coming again. But the reindeer are ready—and on the move!